Contents Page

Introduction

About 8 years ago, my marriage ended, and my life spiralled out of control. In short, it seemed everything I had trusted and believed in had been shattered!

I found myself constantly meeting partners who just could not commit, leading me to ask the question, was it something I was doing?

I found myself searching for answers and in doing so, have slowly had to unpick my own behaviours and patterns, to find answers and determine whether it was something I could change.

This book started out as my nightly writing, a sort of diary of my journey, a bit self-indulgent, possibly, but you know what? I am ok with that. I really hoped to create a short snapshot of how I behave within relationships and determine if this can change.

So here it goes; my name is Maria, and you know what? I am enough, and I like me for who I am, and that is a far cry from how I felt eight years ago.

Different Attachment Styles

Recognising your attachment style is so important, it really plays a big part in how you behave within relationships.

How we attach as adults is shaped by how we attached as a child.

Four distinct styles of attachment have been identified and recognising what pattern you have can be a massive first step to strengthening your relationships.

- Secure- autonomous
- Avoidant- dismissing
- Anxious- preoccupied
- Disorganized- unresolved

It is important to remember you can be different attachment styles, or even more than one attachment style. Moreover, your attachment style can change with different people. For example, an anxious attachment style matched with a secure style could balance out the anxious style person, therefore making them a more secure partner.

below are short outlines of each attachment type:

Secure

Does not display unhealthy, avoidance or anxious traits. Secure patterns do not have unhealthy thoughts of abandonment and tend to be secure in who they are.
Secure patterns are happy to commit and welcome healthy relationships, whereby both partners equally depend on each-other.

Avoidant

Avoids commitment at any cost, generally low on anxiety and is uncomfortable with commitment and relationships, becoming close with others, or partners depending on them.
Values independence, freedom, not needing committed relationship.
Generally, needs to be independent within a relationship and prefers to make decisions alone.

Anxious
Welcomes intimacy and closeness, in fact these are some of the most important things in their relationship. Anxious types often throw themselves into relationships, often losing

themselves along the way as they become so invested in others. Generally, they have fears of abandonment, often leading to partners pulling away. They can be consumed with fears of not being loved, or of not being enough for their partner, and are prone to second guessing themselves.

Disorganised

This pattern often has unresolved issues, emotions and memories, often resulting from unresolved traumas.

Certain issues in their life may not have been resolved, can be reluctant to emotional closeness, argumentative, rages, also can become abusive and unable to regulate emotions leading to depression.

Looking at my own patterns, I believe I have displayed an Anxious style of partnering, and often find myself being drawn to avoidant styles, Seeking validation in my own childhood that all was well, witnessing arguments and feeling helpless to put them right all contributed to the development of this.

My Tender Heart
My Journey Emotional Abuse to Self-Love

Love Bomb

So here I am: It is 5am in the morning and I am texting my ex-sister in law my deepest darkest emotions. Am I crazy? For a while I was starting to think I was, but no, I am not crazy; passionate? Yes. Emotional? Yes. Impulsive? Definitely. 8 years ago, my world fell apart when my husband of more than 20 years had an affair with his colleague. Honestly, I thought I could never feel pain like that again! Fast forward a year whilst standing in a bar I met the man of my dreams... or so I thought. Foreign, silent, brooding and passionate.

And here is where my journey into the emotional roller-coaster starts. At first, he was the perfect guy and understood me so well. The fact that I had come out of a long-term marriage, was going through a messy divorce and had two mature sons did not seem to put him off, even though he was 11 years younger. The sex was amazing, and I felt like his

Superwoman: in loving me he helped me to love myself again. I no longer felt like the discarded woman I had done after discovering my husband's affair. Little did I know then what real emotional mess I was, or what was awaiting me as the months and years passed. Slowly, the lovely gestures turned to small criticisms: "You are quite old "and "You are lucky to have a toy boy" among other slights.

The warning signs were there, but I was willingly blind, or perhaps just naïve. On our third date we went out to a small pub in Kent, and he was quick to remind me: "I am not your boyfriend- we are just friends dating". I remember thinking that was a strange thing to announce but put it down to cultural differences. I was wrong. I later realised that he was most likely on the tail end of another relationship. The poor girl's lipstick and toiletries were still in the bathroom cabinet when I first stayed the night. I asked him who's it was, and he calmly announced that "she was a lodger, more near the end; I asked her to go months before. I was doing her a favour letting her stay and it just

went on too long". Me being me, I believed him-
after all, why would he lie?

The day she came to get her things I sat
outside in my car waiting for her to go, feeling
sorry for her, and wondering why it was all so
secret if she had just been a lodger as he had
said. In retrospect, I now see she was a
discarded lover. Most likely she asked for more
commitment or raised her boundaries, much
like me now.

The Veil Slips

The madness continued and a few months later I found out he had a wife abroad and a potential child! I remember that Saturday morning well; we both sat waiting in the Natural History Museum for his wife and child to arrive. Writing now, I see the absurdity of the arrangement, but at the time no red flag could puncture my blind love.

She approached with her son and a new-born baby in her arms- her new partner beside her. Prior to this meeting he had told me the child was not his, but another man's. Nonetheless, he told me, her family believed it to be his and so he went along with the pretence. Even the boy was unaware; I should have run away then and there, but me being me, I thought I would give him the benefit of the doubt. "We all have baggage", I thought. After all, I was going through a messy divorce myself with 2 teenage sons. Who was I to judge? I remember to this day the look on that woman's face; she still loved this man, even with a new partner and a baby in her arms. I could not help feeling sorry for the guy, as much like me, he probably wondered what the hell he was doing there.

I could see the hope in her eyes that he would still accept the child was his. I could see that she hoped to maintain some connection to him through it. How crazy, I thought, but now I can only imagine the broken promises and dreams she must had endured; how hot and cold he was with her; how he might have punished her with silence amongst other behaviours. And at the end of it all, I witnessed the abandonment. Now I am the victim of the same emotionally draining behaviour. I can only imagine she loved the memory of the guy she married, as that is what abusive behaviour does. It takes the sanest of people and turns their mind inside out. It makes you second guess everything, including your gut instinct. The emotionally avoidant partner very calmly reminds you that you are the crazy one crying all the time. They make you feel guilty when you do not know what you did wrong and make you apologise when it was you who was wronged. All the while they remain perfectly calm- watching and waiting for your apologies.

As for the child, he played the surrogate father figure for a while, but like everything else he tired of the commitment, no more mention of him and no more contact. He was discarded like a toy a child has outgrown. Are you beginning to see the pattern? He loved people if they were not demanding of him and then discarded them like tissues if they were. I remember wanting to ask more questions, but I learnt that there were consequences for asking questions. Moreover, we were now moving into our first year and the mind games had intensified. He would remind me that I was older than him often, said he loved me "anyway", as if there was something shameful about my age difference. As a result, I would always try to look nice, but he would rarely if ever compliment me. He would always

notice a new haircut or dress, but never gave praise. Instead, he would make small, cutting remarks. He might say a certain dress made my backside look big, but then continued to encourage me to eat all the same. He would discreetly flirt with people when we were out, but if I spoke to someone and appeared friendly, even to a friend of his, he would make sarcastic comments and sulk. I felt like he was starting to put me down at every opportunity.

Most people would have walked away by now, but when you are a co-dependant "and I clearly was" you try to fix these issues instead of fleeing. Big mistake. Nights out were normally followed by an argument in

which I always ended up apologising. Most of the time I did not even know what for. He would become silent and "Sorry" was the only way to win his affection back once more.

I never knew how the arguments started most of the time, but he always managed to make me feel it was solely my fault: "You nag me, ask too many questions; It's always 'Why? Why?'." In retrospect, I realise I apologised to maintain a quiet life, but there was a price to pay for this submission. Slowly, my self-esteem started to disappear; I always felt nervous on nights out, and unsure whether I had provoked him. Ultimately, in my attempts to please him, I was losing myself and clearly pushing him further away.

The humiliation grew more frequent. I remember one evening a friend of his turned up at his house with a young girl in her 20's. This friend of his was frequently hostile to me and I got the impression that my partner fed him a narrative that painted me as possessive and unstable. I felt so uncomfortable as the girl circled the living room, clearly drunk and was extremely familiar with both men. To add insult to injury, she turned to me and said wryly: "Nice jacket- my mum has one like that". It was so nasty the way she said it and alongside this cutting remark, she made other comments about my age. The worst thing about it was my partner seemed to enjoy my discomfort and made no attempt to comfort me. Once again, I went home feeling like shit.

After the silence and many tears, I would be forgiven. To achieve this, however, I would have to shut my mouth. This was rewarded with short-lived happy periods where he would shower me with immense love. Though fleeting, I would live for these moments.
At this point I must point out that I am by no means a saint. I can argue and nag as well as anyone. Despite this, I try to forgive and forget, and whereas he put me down, I would seek to

build him up. He, to the contrary, would have me sobbing, broken and begging for
us to make up weekly. I should have walked away but my self-esteem was slowly disappearing. I doubted myself and took his judgments of me as gospel.
Slowly I began to stop feeling like myself anymore.

Many years of this behaviour passed. Parallel to this. I was increasingly trying harder and harder to please him, knowing nothing would ever be good enough. I stopped asking anything from him, even though it was important to me and sacrificed many of my principles and desires to avoid conflict. I stopped asking him to come to family dinners, for instance, as it was only ever met with hostility. He felt under threat from meeting my family, I see this now. I had lost all sense of myself and my happiness now depended on him being in a good or bad mood. Alongside this, his behaviour grew increasingly cold and he grew increasingly distant. I thought if I just tried a bit harder, he would show me the kind gentle man I craved, but this was not what happened. His affection had become like a drug and I would literally shake inside when he went cold on me. I felt so alone I craved his affection. Looking back, I felt he weaponised love to keep me in line.

I think it was a Saturday morning when I woke up, still going through my messy divorce and feeling completely overwhelmed by the ongoing legal battle. For context, my ex-husband was using delaying tactics and hiding his financial situation from me and my solicitor. I was on a basic income- about to be on the breadline once my meagre savings had run out and my ex did not want me to
take a penny of his pensions. He had a new younger model to maintain now and saw me as a burden.

I remember turning to my new partner and saying, exasperated: "God, I cannot fight anymore, he can keep everything, I just want peace". He looked back at me, no comforting arm or tender look offered and said bluntly: "Maria, you are weak, and you need to be strong. "What would you do on your own without me".   I remember how those words cut deeply. At first, I was angry for his lack of comfort and support, but then I wondered whether he was right. By telling me I was weak

I felt like I needed him more; he was so stoic, and nobody got the better of his emotions- not his family and certainly not me.

The divorce had taken its toll on me and I started to believe I was nothing on my own; the message had been reinforced in me so many times that I felt worthless, spurned and undesirable, mainly on account of my age. "Younger is better" had been drilled into me by the Media and every man I had loved. "You're getting old, you can't do that alone" I told myself. I was willing to accept anything if it kept me from being alone.

The divorce finally came through after years of back and forth. I remember feeling total relief. There was no bitterness or anger anymore- just relief. I thought to myself how happy me and my partner could now be together (here the need to be attached and safe again). For years he had said, time and time again, that he did not like the fact that I was still married and tied to my ex in name and law, even though he had made no attempt to end his own marriage (his reason being he needed to go to Brazil to do it). Like everything else, I just accepted it. It was one rule for him and another for me. I was sure that now my situation had changed, he would be happy, and we could finally have a normal life together.

Divorce done; it was not long before he found new reasons to become avoidant. There were wants and desires that I could not satisfy and which he resented me for. He wanted another child and constantly spoke of this. This was cruel on his part, especially as he knew I could not do this now that I was over 50 and undergoing the menopause. Of course, he knew this when he met me, but it did not stop him from holding it over my head. He continued to make comments: "If you had a baby when we met, I would not be feeling like this now" he would say. I started to feel old and guilty all over again and when I told him this, he would become distant with me, followed with more late-night drinking sessions. He would go off radar, turn his phone off and would be avoidant if I questioned why.

He said he was getting a fertility test, and dependent on the result; if he were fertile, he would find another life away from me, if not, he would stay. He was rolling some dice on our relationship and I believe saw me as a backup plan. Again, I should have raised my boundaries and fled, but my self-worth was all but gone.

So many times, I planned how great life was going to be, and daydreamed about a future where he would lift me from my humdrum existence (again here I am waiting to be rescued). Sometimes, I even planned it on a picture board, with goals, targets and timelines. I was addicted to his promises and dependent on his validation, but it was so unpredictable. Years of this took its toll; his constant avoidant behaviour, the starving of affection and the silent treatment were taking their toll on me. I learned to sense when I was about to be put through the wringer so to speak; he would become cold, distant and strangely calm. When I saw the signs, it made me feel nervous and queasy. There had been so many occasions- too many to write about- but some stand out and emotionally scarred me inside like nothing you can imagine. More than anything, however, these years were defined by that strange sick feeling of love being torn apart.

Over the following months YouTube relationship self-help videos became my new best friend, alongside every self-help Audio book I could find on relationships, emotional abuse and gaslighting. I just needed to know that I was not going crazy. When he was kind and loving I felt guilty for saying he was avoidant and cold, but when the mask slipped and he punished me with silence, it seemed clear that he was.

He felt that I was damaged from my marriage and that it was me who needed help. Repeatedly he drilled it into me that I was the problem and slowly but surely, I believed him. Inside, I could not shake this feeling that something was off, but I had stopped trusting my own instincts and judgements. I should have been kinder to myself, but I did not love myself enough to listen to that little inner voice. When you lose all self-worth and stop believing in your own judgements, you become vulnerable to manipulation.

When life is running smoothly, I am quite secure and focused, so I ask the question: Can we have more than one style of attachment? I believe we can, and that it is dependent on who you are partnered with, in my case with an avoidant, which seems to have been the problem for our relationship. As someone with an anxious attachment relationship type I need reassurance, security, and stability; all the things that make an avoidant run for cover.

In short, I am facing the fact that I have anxious traits, and in a way, it feels comforting to know why I behave the way I do. By understanding the causes of my anxious attachment style, I have developed new, healthier working models of behaviour.

Mum's Decline

My mother was nearing the end and had grown
frail; it was a draining time for me and my
sisters and naturally I turned to my partner for
emotional support. Instead of offering this, he
recoiled from me and except for a few kind
gestures, was quite avoidant.

I remember so many times in the past I had
wanted him to come to family gatherings, but he
never had time; not even to pop in briefly. If I
persistently asked, I knew already, cold silence,
no contact and talk of leaving me. If I argued
my point and I often tried to, we would go
straight to drunken night out with his friends and
no communication, but always I was left
begging and apologising. I would ask questions
and yes, I would get upset at the lack of
empathy or care, but if we had communicated
better it all could have been avoided, that was
never an option.

He always managed to make me feel it was my
fault, and mostly it was always me that had to
apologise and take blame, I should have left
then I know that now, stood my ground,

withheld better boundaries, but like so many times before I really did start to believe it was all me and he was so convincing in his argument.

I remember thinking to myself, on so many occasions who will want a 50 something year old woman, with all my emotional baggage, something he would regularly remind me of. At the same time my sister number 3, who was now in a nursing home with Multiple Sclerosis had become ill again , it was a heavy time what with mum and it played on my mind daily that everyone around me was ill or dying. He seemed like my only light at times, so alive. I remember trying to discuss the matter of my sister many times, and asked him once if he would come to the home with me to see her, I remember his faced dropped and I got a blunt NO, I don't want to be around sickness and negativity, I felt so lonely at times, this was my sister after all.

Over time it become clear he had no interest to meet my friends and family or attending any gatherings or get togethers that should have been a red flag right there, but I did not want to believe it. What really hurt was I had visited his parents a year before his grandmother a lovely older woman had severe dementia she would curse and shout all day long , I embraced the situation as did he so clearly he knew how to show kindness around sick people, only just for me he would not make that kind of commitment.

Relationships really need to be an even measure of give and take, when things are unbalanced, something will always give, that said at some point, all relationships can

become unbalanced.   One or the other parties may have a crisis or drama, but this should not be the norm long term, otherwise quiet resentment sets in and for me it had.

That is the problem being an anxious pleaser, the one who always gives, if you are unable to discuss and express yourself for fear of losing someone, eventually you lose yourself, boundaries are crossed and respect is lost for yourself and from others.

I would always justify everything, by telling myself we cannot all be the same, the world needs people like me, the ones that do not rock

the boat, who just do regardless of how shit it makes
us feel. But you know what? The world does not need you to be a door mat, the thing is if we do not make our own boundaries, who will?
And in time, we slowly lose ourselves.

4am My old Friend

I look at my watch, it is 4am, I barely slept again, this is becoming my new normal. It is a strange feeling, I have gone past feeling tired, just empty and numb, it seems the only thing to do is write. Funny thing about putting thoughts down on paper, as if all the bad energy, anger, frustration and sadness, sinks into the words on the paper for a small while dulls this unbearable pain.

Before I woke tonight, I dreamt again about him of course, going over what happened even in my sleep, my head trying to find a grain of truth, something real and meaningful in the years we have spent together. Now it all feels like a bad dream, only to wake and find my real life is the nightmare, filled with sadness and rejection.

I feel so anxious tonight, I scramble in the dark to find my phone, tapping in meditation to sleep, after a short while of breathing exercises and calming mantra, I feel a gentle calm wash over me.

How did I get here? This is the question I constantly keep asking myself. Ok, well my marriage ended, big mess, but not actually, I had two fantastic sons and mostly an honest run at marriage, even if the end was a bit crap. But hey ho shit happens, people fall in and out of love, so why has this last relationship jarred me so badly? Honestly, I think it is the emotional games, the silence and the ability he had to manipulate me, believing anything he said was right.

But I guess I really need to have a conversation with myself at this point, I was a strong-minded woman, who got through a messy divorce, heartbreaks, family crisis, deaths numerous disappointments, so how did I become such a vulnerable, anxious mess? God I am tired as my alarm beeps 6am, time for work and again, the cycle begins.

I stumble downstairs, almost breaking my neck on the dog, I am determined to pull myself together, so I get onto the exercise bike 20 mins of sweat and crying, all at the same time, I am getting really good at this multitasking grief whilst maintain a routine, I pop on my gel eye mask so as I cry, my eyes do not swell, bloody hell I think I really have lost the plot!

Honestly, I cannot tell you one thing about my day at work, other than I was there, I smiled and laughed, whilst this mass of emotion sat inside of me. I longed to look at my phone and just see one message from him. I was like an addict. I needed my fix, but nothing, I felt dead inside.

Little Anxious Me

3am another bad dream, I awake sweating. I had been dreaming again, always the same anxious pit in my stomach when I wake, It was quite surreal, but as I looked around the room just me and the dog, snoring gently outside the door, a deep slumber that I can only dream of.

I started to think back to when I was a child, and how I wanted so much for everything to be perfect, like on the TV shows, but of course it was not, don't get me wrong I was loved, I knew this, but family life was chaotic, even a bit bonkers at times.
Mum love her, was agoraphobic, she did not like outsiders or people who were not family or familiar coming to the house. This was probably due to her childhood of being fostered, too many people who did not really want her, they were not kind to her at all.
 Dad however was different; he loved a drink and a party.

As a child I remember that sick nervous feeling in my stomach, the one he gives me, now I really hate that feeling, a sickening dread, it scares me, I know what will follow.
I knew as we left family gatherings, dad more than merry again, mum bless her sober, disappointed and ready to go, I knew it would not be a quiet night.

I remember one night among many, pots and pans would crash, harsh words exchanged, shouting and a lot of tears. My sisters saw more, me being the youngest, I suppose I was protected a bit, nonetheless it impacted on me. Soon to follow was bed wetting, and various problems at school, for years I struggled. Another night of mum and dad shouting and screaming, dad had been out to drink again and had rode his bike home drunk, it all went quiet, eventually everyone went to bed.

 I could not sleep, I just used to cry, I remember, on several occasions, I would crawl into bed with mum, some ungodly hour with the intention to make her feel better. Of course, the last thing she wanted was a clingy child, when all she really dreamed of was running away, I just made her more upset, I felt so sad inside and helpless, I could never make it ok.

Fast forward a few more years, by this time I had worked out a strategy to avoid all the drama. I would seek refuge at my best friend at schools house, whose family were not perfect by any stretch of the imagination, but for me, it was heaven; they laughed and joked, ate together- free in so many ways I was not.

I spent more and more of my time there. Her mum and dad never married, quite unusual in my family, as marriage was what happens before children, or so I grew up to believe. This aside, the union between her mum and dad, had been one with much love.
I loved my hours at their house as it was free of shouting and arguments.

Negative Attachment

I honestly believe this is where my Anxious attachment style really started to grow wings. You see, mum was anxious/avoidant, and although loving in her own way, she was dealing with her own demons, and really did not have time to notice that I was falling apart.
In no way am I blaming this all on mum, she parented to the best of her ability, with the lessons she had learnt. For Mum. being fed, warm, and surrounded by family, was all you needed.

Education was not her priority, why would it be.? She was not taught that lesson.
Dad was much the same, he worked hard, paid mum all the money each week, provided for us, but pretty much did his own thing. Both worked hard, they never wanted us to go without anything, but the emotional stuff was so critical I craved that re-assurance, and it was never verbally talked about, I had to make my own story, and I made a negative one.

Anyway, let me continue…

I went home from school much like I always did that day, I remember dad just sitting at the kitchen table, vest on like always, much like the Brazilian wife at the museum that day, lost in thought but pained. Something was wrong; there it was again, that sick nervous feeling in my stomach: "mums gone", he said. I remember asking a hundred questions at once. what, where, why? But there were no answers. I was starting to raise my voice and cry at this point, "she's gone- I don't know where, and I am not sure when she's coming back ".

I remember calling her all sorts of names, I could not understand when dad lost his temper, and smacked me hard round my face: "don't speak about your mother like that" he said. I ran upstairs and locked myself away. My sister was equally as shocked, bless her; she took the brunt of it all really.

I have three sisters, two had already left home so that left me, and sister number two, the two youngest left behind at home in the chaos, that was to become our life, I remember they were strange times and all a bit of a blur really.

Looking back now that is when this journey of looking for happiness in others started, like where's Walley, but instead of a red bobble hat, I looked for fun, laughter and excitement in every crowd I found myself. I was starting to be quite the woman at this point, so it was not hard for me to attract all the wrong kind of attention, I did not care if it was exciting, fun and fast, anything but sadness and arguments.

So many years were spent like this; running from one dysfunctional relationship to another, they were not bad people, just damaged like me I suppose.

I realised very quickly, the damaged find the damaged like little home fires, we just seem to know when we meet another; pain feels others pain.

I remember the time I met the boxer. He was loud, wild and exciting. We locked eyes and life was never going to be the same again. I was young and stupid and whilst intoxicating, it was all a bit dysfunctional.

I can honestly say I have been in real love 3 times in my life, well that's if you don't count my kids, and closest friends because that is also falling in love, but without the sex.

My first real love was the boxer, we had many years of crazy making, but a lot of laughs too, and we remain good friends today.
The second my husband, well that was my one sensible phase, out of all my lovers he was stable, I went for what was good for me for once, well I would not have had kids if he had not been.

We had a lot of good years, many fantastic adventures, as we travelled a lot with our young children, we did a fairly good job of our marriage for over 20 years, don't get me wrong, it was not all rosy, there were dark times too, but overall I found some calm and stability, I craved this, the shy anxious little girl inside needed this and my marriage did not disappoint for many years.

My marriage was considered to be one of the strongest by the school gate mums, "how funny", I used to think, people really do only see what they want sometimes, but that said, we were never the couple that sat in silence across from one another; we always had conversation, my marriage was working, until one day it didn't anymore.

I am not sure why it all went so wrong really, but he did have the affair, so I blamed him, but in all honesty, inside of myself I still missed the excitement and the drama,
We had become, like most parents with young kids, set in our routines and lazy to each other's needs and before long, resentment sets in. I am sure this is a story many married couples with kids can relate to.

It was messy and sad near the end of my marriage; the divorce dragged on for so many years, and eventually, after too many harsh words and broken promises, we both walked away. For me, it felt we had torn apart the only real stability I had known. This was followed by dark times, depression, a lot of drinking, late nights, weekends out, all between sharing my youngest son with his dad.
I was determined not to let the kids see the drama, not the way I had, sadly, I feel they did a little, and yes, it probably affected them, as much as arguments in my childhood had me.

Dizzy and falling

I was getting ready, another endless night out with friends to drink, party, and to forget my divorce to be honest.

I remember feeling bloody awful, but just put it down to another toxic exchange with my ex-husband, as we had become increasingly hostile with each other, divorce does that, love gone, just the bare truth; love is so fragile at times.

Anyway, off I went into the night to meet my girlfriends, little did I know what was about to unfold.

All I want to say about this time was the night came and by the time it went, I was left with missing teeth, broken ribs and a face worthy of ten rounds with Tyson.

I woke in a pool of my own blood, I had passed out it seems at the top of the stairs,

The following months were terrifying, as doctors started to look at what had caused me to keep feeling dizzy, vomiting, and fainting on a regular basis.

I was convinced I had Multiple Sclerosis, the same illness as my sister. Bloody hell-discarded and now alone to die, great!

A year later I was diagnosed with Meniere's disease, which came as a relief; although debilitating, it is nothing compared with MS.

My anxiety levels rose, I desperately wanted to meet someone, before it was too late, I could not bear to be alone, my whole life I had managed to attach to someone, I needed this, or so I thought.

I have learnt one thing from all these hospital appointments alone; I can only really count on one person to take care of me and that is myself.

I just wish I had known that at the time, but clearly, I had to suffer a little more before that lesson would sink in.

Graduation Day

My youngest had his graduation day, a happy time yes, overshadowed by our never-ending divorce. We had already seen our eldest graduate a few years before, and that all went ok I guess; however, the divorce had taken its toll as it had been rolling on for several years at this point. During this time there were arguments over pensions, the dog, university fees, and pretty much everything really, so I felt a little nervous, especially as my mother in law was here from abroad to join us for the happy day.

I had always got along with my mother-in-law, however like all mothers her loyalty was with her son, if nothing else I could understand that bond; I feel fiercely about my own sons, so it's normal, I guess.

The moment we all came together my husband frantically dashed off to quiet corners to take calls- I am guessing from work and his woman. He was always a workaholic, much like my last partner, and although different in many ways, they were both driven to be the best at what they did. I admired that quality, and if I am honest, wish I had more of their get up and go about myself, I seemed to limp along in life happy to please, doing the running around whilst others shine. With my husband I played the traditional homemaker whilst he gained his qualifications and moved on and with my new partner it was the same, although he did not commit, and we did not share a home together.

I could not help looking around at all the families together that day, united, or so it seemed, you see this is typical of me, always thinking everyone else's life is perfect, when of course, I know it is not, probably each family here had their own baggage, much like our family.

It really is important to not measure your worth or your life by others; you will most certainly only ever see their positives, and your negatives. You must run your own race. This is an area I am working on daily, as when your self-worth is low it is so easy to let that inner voice destroy you. I spent a lot of time that day, my little inner voice chanting in my head, "thank you for my sons and all the things that I am blessed for". It was a happy day and I felt proud for the beautiful men I have been blessed to have in my life, my sons.

The final blow

I know this is sounding like a diary of my life, and yes I guess it is a little, however for you to get a clear picture of how I became attached, without clear boundaries, I feel I need to go over my journey, as each step has brought me to this moment.

So here we are again; it is 3am and my mind is racing like an out of control steam train, sleeping tablets were not even working at this point, and as a result my sleep pattern was erratic, so I decided to write.

I'm sat here, pen to paper, in the hope of halting my sad thoughts, my dog jumps up beside me, he is particularly knowing tonight, his little face almost willing me: "come on, you can do this" as he gently licks my hand. Bugger it, I will do this...! Strangely I do not feel alone anymore, I have a feeling of calm, it seems to surround me, strange in that moment, I know what I need to do.

For the first time in 54 years, I feel a real connection between everything I have endured; heartbreak, seeing the people I love slowly waste away, it had led me to this point, maybe my nightly writing, my inner most thoughts, could help another? Just maybe there is another tender heart out there right now, suffering, willing somebody to help ease that sickening pain inside as I have felt so many nights in silence, alone.

Two months I have not been with him now, we made some contact, he had texted me that he has been in tears, sad, and missing me beyond belief, so we decided to meet. It was a strange feeling, almost like meeting a stranger to be honest, but we warmed as the hours passed and the evening ended well. We departed with a kiss and kind words.

The following day he was silent again; I felt such fool. Why I do never learn?

The time away from him was awful. I can honestly say I can imagine what a drug addict feels like as the comedown from his love was breathtakingly painful. My mind drifted back to that last evening out before he discarded me. In retrospect, I should have seen it coming really, we had an evening planned with family and friends in another local bar.

As the evening ended, he walked me to my car and said goodnight; I remember that kiss was so tender, different from the last few months, almost like he knew what was about to happen, and showing me one last farewell. Saturday again, he had his breakfast and ran much like every other weekend. I went shopping and, on my return, checked my phone; I looked at Facebook. His post had a different feel, not his usual stuff, all love, hearts and glitter.

My curiosity got the better of me, so I looked at a few comments, BAM! there it was, funny how fate plays its hand sometimes, I clicked on a comment, there she was, a love interest from two years ago, Miss Hello Trouble, my heart sank- a horrible feeling- whilst panic and anxiety washed over me. I clicked on her homepage only to see they had gone into business together; it read a collaboration of 2 years in progress, I felt physically sick.

I immediately texted him, but as always, his response was calm and read "its business, nothing"

I remember the next day going to his flat, I wanted to confront him, I needed answers, all I remember, that he was cold, cutting, what had I done to deserve this? I lashed out, a real girly slap, I know I should not have, honestly, I was in shock, I felt that familiar, deep despair, wash over me.

My Aha! Moment

What followed I will never forget, the feeling of awful shame, intense pain and utter loneliness.

I drove to his house and confronted him. It was a moment, but how do you justify yourself, here I was in his home, a woman in her 50's , it would have sounded crazy if I had tried to explain to anyone, the years of mental torture, the "I love you'" ,followed by years of broken promises.

Over the coming weeks I spiralled into a deep depression which engulfed me. One night, I remember contemplating how I could end everything, but I quickly pulled myself back, my inner voice screaming, "Selfish Bitch". I thought of all the people I would hurt, people who really cared about me, and my son finding me.

I pulled myself together, poured a glass of wine, and started listening to my audio books; it was by a woman who had been subjected to

Narcissistic abuse in her relationship. Her words really hit me as she described the

"compliments laced with shit ". Yes, this sums up how I felt perfectly; he always gave me half compliments laced with shit...!! Still my craving for the life with him is still strong, I know its toxic, at times, I know I have suffered, but still, I miss him. However, that said, I miss me more, and this time I choose me.

Here is my theory, when you have a good heart, a tender loving heart, you always look within before blaming others, and that's no bad thing, however there must come a time when we love ourselves too.
We must become our own protector, or we will disappear, only to become nothing, and for what? Another's ego.

I needed to write this brief experience for anyone else out there that is in this abusive web, and to tell you: You may not leave today, or tomorrow, but please try to love you, find the strength to escape the crazy making and stop allowing another to put out the light on your beautiful soul. As for him or her even, are they an evil person? No, not at all. Ambitious yes, determined at any cost, yes, avoidant, I believe so, however that being said, there are many people, some in positions of power, who are no different from him.

That said, mental abuse is wrong; to knowingly do it, or to keep another down to feed your own ego, this is wrong, but I truly believe that behind the tough exterior he is a scared child, damaged by his own demons. That said, they were and are his demons, not mine...!

The lesson? When confronted by a damaged person, do not try to fix them, especially if they do not want to be fixed, as you will only lose yourself, and your kind heart will suffer in the process.

Support them, guide them and if that is not enough, detach from them. Of course, this is easier said than done, and will take time, but educating yourself, learning new paths and strengthening your boundaries is a journey and not an overnight job.

Healthy Life/Relationship Rules

- "By becoming aware of your attachment style, both you and your partner can challenge the insecurities and fears supported by your age-old working models and develop new styles of attachment for sustaining a satisfying, loving relationship."

- Do not place all your self- worth in another person as it is not healthy or sustainable and love yourself before looking for love from others. On this point, a relationship should be something you choose to be in because you enjoy each other's company. It should never be something you need.

- It is believed that great wisdom in relationships comes with age, and therefore, we do not make the same old mistakes, Well, mistakes are part of life and are essential for growth, at any age. Love is a skill, and it is only by learning from our mistakes that we can get better at it.

- Learn to celebrate your flaws and imperfections, after all, they make you who you are; only once you learn to love every part of yourself, can you truly learn to love another.

- Try to live every day in the here and now, live for the moment, and take one day at a time, this way you will not overwhelm yourself. In short, daily small steps are better than huge leaps, and will leave you less likely to fail.

- Laugh at everything, even the moments that broke you, because they are just moments, and as quick as they break us, we can learn to move forward, making us so much stronger and resilient.

I aim to work on myself daily, for however long I am blessed to stay here. Each day is my classroom, and I will do my best to embrace every obstacle and to keep growing.

At some point you will be ready to find love again after suffering emotional abuse. This can feel very daunting, and you will have fears and worries that you could be manipulated again. I honestly believe you need to feel that fear of rejection and embrace it, and to remember that not all relationships are going to be lasting. However, if that should happen, this is a good opportunity to use these experiences as a learning ground where you can grow through these situations. In the end, they will undoubtedly make you stronger.

Of course it is a good idea to be in a better head space before we dip our toes again, however saying that, there will never be a perfect time or day to do this; from experience, it's just not how it works I am afraid to say.

If you are aware of your attachment style and own your insecurities, be aware you that you cannot rely on another to fill you up and make you feel fully secure.
Yes, of course if a partner is over-critical or not willing to equally nurture the relationship, this is a red flag and that it is the time to step back and decide if we want to continue, set some

ground rules and mean them. If that person is willing to work from this point then that is great, if not, it might be time to walk away.

Choose people that choose you, and by this, I mean make sure potential partners are equally invested from the start. Word of advice: Put yourself in the more important position at the beginning until you get to know a partner a little more.
It may take time for you to learn these skills whilst dating again, and to not invest too quickly, especially if somebody seems too good to be true. In short, enjoy the moment, but invest in you first and take things at a slower pace; if somebody truly cares enough that they want to get to know you better they will be willing to wait a little and give you that time and space.

If you do find yourself feeling anxious or desperate you may lose the potential partner if you do not travel at their pace, ask your inner voice (that inner child) where most of these fears originated from. Perhaps it is connected to past fears, in which case, nurture that inner voice and in time, it will grow in strength and the anxious voice inside will calm.

Something that works well for me is to give myself 15 minutes before you send that desperate text or make that phone call; breathe deeply and start a dialogue with that inner voice. This often this helps me to make better choices.

Another trait I found myself exhibiting as an anxious type was that I often made grand gestures, many of which were not appreciated or reciprocated, and I would find myself feeling underappreciated and exploited as a result. If this sounds like you, ask yourself an honest question: Are you making grand gestures out of an abundance of love with no expectation? Or is this action to feed your ego and make that person like or love you more? It's a great feeling to give our partners gifts and spoil them if this action is coming from a loving place with shared values, but if you find yourself doing this purely to please, understand this pattern and look to change it. It is no fun to do things for another when it stems from the desire to receive validation of your relationship. This will only lead to resentment and disappointment in the end. Let me clarify, this is not to say your partner should not be appreciative of your kind gestures, but make sure that they come from the right place.

It is important to remember not to abandon yourself to others desires and needs; self-love is not just about taking long walks and bubble baths; it also involves practicing self-discipline. Moreover, self-love consists of pushing yourself to reach goals, and to not be distracted by other's needs. Self-love can sometimes mean being less self-indulgent, and on occasions giving yourself a good talking to. Sometimes this may feel like uncomfortable, but only when we start to push our self and value our worth will our self-esteem start to grow.

In my experience, amazing things can happen when you stretch yourself; your boundaries naturally start to raise up, and you naturally become less tolerant of those who constantly see you as an easy target.

Sometimes we may have to let certain people in our life go, but you know what? That is ok, however, saying that, in my experience the ones that are worthwhile often return and adjust to your new style.

You may even find that a relationship where you had low boundaries can be salvaged after time apart and a good deal of work on both sides. It takes time for reconciliation if there has been emotional abuse in a relationship, and both parties must want change and be fully committed to this long term.

In every relationship, no matter our attachment style, there will be times when we all experience pain and disappointment. But when we have these moments, it's important to sit with that pain and to process it; only when we can do this can we really get a hold on our relationship with others and most importantly, our self.

Finding Self Love

These dark months during the breakup, I remember walking a lot. I did not have a destination, I just enjoyed each step and kept walking, meditating, and clearing my busy mind. Sometimes we need a little more help for a while, mine were sleeping aids, which were carefully prescribed by my doctor, I honestly think if I endured any more sleepless nights, I would have become seriously ill. It's important to care for yourself in whatever form that takes, be it exercise, walking, seeing friends, and even medication temporarily; antidepressants have their place, and can keep you afloat until the path ahead becomes a little lighter to walk.

I cannot express enough the importance of my daily walks in nature; just to breath and walk is therapy, and it will ground you and make you feel stronger. At my lowest point, a good friend arranged a mindful forest walk; she never told me about it, but just texted out of the blue: "I will pick you up at 9". I may have been resistant if I had known, but I can never thank her enough for that morning as it really did set me on my path to recovery, and gave me the push I needed to really open up this behaviour once and for all. I will be eternally grateful to her for that.

So here I am, laid bare. It is said everybody experiences some damage in their life, so I do not want to sound like a victim I am not. I made most of my bad choices, I just hope by sharing my experiences I will help at least one person to see a way out, or at least offer some peace of mind that they are not alone or going mad.

Continuing, not all abuse is visible; the scars of emotional abuse are internal, and are brought on by another's actions, words and behaviours. If you are, as I am, an anxious attachment, it can in some cases damage so much more, as its invisible to those around you. Be kind to yourself, take a small step, reach out to loved ones and find your way.

But the question is: Can you change your relationships patterns? Or can we untangle our learnt behaviours? In short, I believe we can, but only if we are willing to work on ourselves. With honest self-evaluation and a desire to change, your attachment style can be overcome and transformed over time, although this will not be a quick process. Moreover, research has shown that an anxious or avoidant personality who enters a long-tern relationship with a secure can be elevated to the level of the secure over time. It light of this, it might be wise to choose your partners carefully also.

So here I am, a work in progress; I believe I will always have a little anxiety as it is in my nature, but slowly I am making better choices, raising my boundaries and growing one day at a time. Here is to all you tender beautiful people, who have loved deeply and unconditionally, remember: Always love yourself, because true love is an inside job.

All My Love

Maria x

And on this my last page, I would like to thank my closest companion, who loyally snuggled at the end of my bed throughout the tears and shared so many painful moments, who sat and endured so much pain and heartache by my side, be it relationship breakups, death or health scares. This is for you my little Russell. With love and hugs x. 🖤

Printed in Great Britain
by Amazon